WHEN THE TOM-TOM BEATS

WHEN THE TOM-TOM BEATS

Selected Prose & Poems

by Jacques Roumain

Translated by Joanne Fungaroli
& Ronald Sauer

Introduction by
Paul Laraque

Azul Editions
MCMXCV

This bilingual edition is published by
Azul Editions
2032 Belmont Rd., N.W.
Suite 301
Washington, D.C. 20009
USA

Front cover batik: *The Drummer* (1988) © Paul Nzalamba
(Los Angeles, CA)

ISBN 0-9632363-8-5
Library of Congress Catalog Number: 94-72476

Printed in the United States of America

First Edition
10 9 8 7 6 5 4 3 2 1

CONTENTS

INTRODUCTION

Although Jacques Roumain lived but 37 years (1907-1944), during his lifetime he was a journalist, politician, diplomat, professor, ethnographer, poet, short story writer, novelist and revolutionary.

Born in Port-au-Prince on 4 June 1907, Roumain was still a boy when the "blancs" landed in Haiti in 1915. Charlemagne Péralte, leader of the peasant rebellion against the American military occupation, was assassinated in 1919. He was succeeded by his second-in-command, Benoit Batraville, who was killed in combat in 1920. It was during that same year that the thirteen-year-old Roumain was sent to Switzerland to complete his education at the Institut Grunau in Berne, in keeping with the Haitian élite's tradition of sending its children to Europe to complete their formal education. After six years living and studying in Switzerland, France, Germany and Spain, Jacques left off with his studies and returned to his homeland, committed to fight in the cause of Haitian nationalism. Roumain immediately joined the vanguard of the resistance movement against the American occupation and was soon elected president of the Haitian Patriotic Youth League, the organization primarily responsible for the eventual end to the U.S. occupation.

In 1927, Roumain co-founded, along with Philippe Thoby-Marcelin, Carl Brouard and Antonio Vieux, *La Revue Indigène: Les Arts et la Vie,* the journal that opened the period of modern poetry and literature in our country and gave voice to the politic of the newly formed Indigenous Movement. Searching for a patriotic Haitian identity as well as for the forms of cultural resistance to the U.S. occupation, the Indigenous Movement did not take long to situate itself within the militant pacifism of labor strikes and public demonstrations. Roumain was arrested and imprisoned. It was during this time that he wrote several literary works, including four short stories under the title *La Proie et l'ombre* (1930) (The Prey and the Shadow), prefaced by Antonio Vieux; *Les Fantouches* (1931) (The Puppets), a scathing indictment of urban collaborative society; and *La Montagne ensorcelée* (1931) (The Bewitched Mountain), a peasant narrative and masterpiece of Roumain's Indigenous period, prefaced by Jean Price-Mars. While these early works depict the decadent Haitian urban élite and the tragic reality of rural Haiti gripped by superstition and fear, they do not — and cannot, as yet — offer a way out.

Roumain's political development continued to evolve until, after the departure of the U.S. Marines in 1934 and their replacement by the "Garde d'Haiti," a native occupation troop, he founded the Communist Party in Haiti and in the same year published *Analyse schématique 1932/1934* (The Schematic Analysis 1932/1934), the first Marxist analysis of Haitian reality. In it a case is made for a Marxist interpretation of Haitian reality, propounding that "with the arrival of the power of the nationalists began the process of nationalism's decay. The reason for this phenomenon is simple: at its base was an anti-imperialist and therefore anti-capitalist movement, and at its top was a petty-bourgeois and bourgeois leadership. Thus nationalism contained internal contradictions that unavoidably caused its own disintegration." With *Analyse schématique 1932/1934* forming the demarcation line between Roumain's Indigenous and Communist periods, he now set his sights on Socialism that, through the struggle of a revolutionary organization, would open the path of liberation for all Haitians. Roumain was now a committed communist in both his thought and his actions, for Marxism was the only ideology that he could envisage as providing a genuine solution to Haiti's class and color conflicts. In 1934, the presidency of Sténio Vincent was swift and brutal in its response to Roumain and the Communist Party. Roumain was arrested and imprisoned for three years for subversive activities. In 1936, with his health failing, he was released and sent into exile.

In exile, Roumain traveled widely in Europe. He studied anthropology at the Sorbonne in Paris, pursuing his passionate interest in peasant culture. He went to Spain with other writers and intellectuals from around the globe in defense of culture against Fascism. His poem "Madrid" is a powerful testament to the human wave of solidarity to defend the Republic against the Fascist onslaught. At the outbreak of the Second World War, Roumain left for the United States and renewed his anthropology studies at Columbia University in New York. It was here that he began his long and close friendship with Langston Hughes. In 1939, he published *Griefs de l'homme noir* (Grievances of the Black Man), a class analysis of racism and the black man in the southern United States. In this clear-sighted book, Roumain has this to say about lynching in the South:

The lyncher is also a victim of the lynching. The mobs that pursue the human "game" are composed of poor whites whose material condition is hardly better than that of the blacks. They labor under the illusion of white superiority and think they have something in common with the ruling classes. Color prejudice is a divisive tool among the workers of the South, whose common revolt could shake the established economic structure.

With the defeat of Vincent by Elie Lescot in the 1941 presidential election, Roumain was permitted to return to Haiti. In no time he founded the *Bureau d'Ethnologie* as a way of institutionalizing the permanent study of Haitian peasant culture. It was at this time that the Catholic Church was waging a vigorous "anti-superstition campaign" to convert Haitian worshippers of the voodoo deities. Roumain was quick to make known his opposition to this religious campaign, and in 1942 he published his essay entitled *Autour de la campagne anti-superstitieuse,* in which he makes his position on the matter plain:

> The essential thing is not to make the peasant renounce his belief in Ogoun. It is rather a question of completely changing his conception of the world . . . . The element of moral coercion used in this campaign is fear. But fear of hell fire has not radically changed their religious view of the world. They have not renounced their belief in the "loas" only their serving of these gods . . . . If one really wishes to change the archaic religious mentality of our peasants, we must educate them. And they cannot be educated unless their material conditions are transformed. Until we have developed a system of rural clinics, the peasant will continue to consult his "bocor" (priest). What we must have in Haiti is not an "anti-superstition campaign" but an "anti-misery campaign."

In 1943, President Lescot appointed Roumain chargé d'affaires at the Haitian embassy in Mexico. Though at first reluctant to accept the post, he went to Mexico at the urging of the Communist Party, which desired to place its members in positions of influence. In Mexico, Roumain perhaps enjoyed the creative freedom he had never known before: he completed the collection of poems *Bois d'ébène* (*Ebony Wood*), included here in its entirety, and his classic novel *Gouverneurs de la rosée* (*Masters of the Dew*). The poems in *Ebony Wood* transform racial solidarity, as advocated by Negritude, into the class solidarity of all peasants and workers regardless of color, as declared by Marxism. Here, poetry aims not only to be beautiful, but also a combat weapon:

Africa I kept your memory Africa
you are in me
Like a splinter in the wound
Like a guardian fetish in the village center
make of me your catapult stone
of my mouth the lips of your wound
of my knees the broken columns of your abasement

BUT

I only want to be of your race
workers peasants of all countries

At the heart of the system that inextricably combines capitalism and racism, the globalizing concept of class integrates social reality's particular aspects: race, ethnicity, religion and culture. Born into a bourgeois mulatto family, Roumain removed himself from the interests of his class to embrace the interests of the masses and the nation. Class consciousness is registered in the struggle for freedom.

Both *Ebony Wood* and *Masters of the Dew* were published posthumously by Roumain's widow shortly after his sudden death on 18 August 1944 in Mexico. *Masters of the Dew* was then translated into Spanish by Nicolás Guillén and into English by Langston Hughes and Mercer Cook. Today, it is still in print in fifteen languages.

At this turning point in our history, the army/police and its hired assassins that serve the oligarchy and imperialism have thwarted the democratic movement set in motion by our people from 1986 to this day. Considering Jean Bertrand Aristide's accession to power and the military coup d'état that overthrew him, the people's organized resistance remains the guarantee of the nation's future. Amilcar Cabral, hero and martyr of the African Marxist guerrilla movement, warns us,

"Only societies which preserve their culture are capable of mobilizing and organizing the masses against foreign domination." Following the torches of Accau,* Péralte, Alexis and Roumain, the struggle will continue by all means — peaceful if possible, violent if necessary — for the second independence, democracy and socialism.

Paul Laraque
New York, 29 April 1994

---

* Jean-Jacques Accau, leader of the 1843 peasant revolt, set forth four basic principles that remain valid for the Haitian democratic revolution: agrarian reform, food self-sufficiency, priority of class issues over race issues, and a popular army.

THE EARLY & MIDDLE POEMS

LE CHANT DE L'HOMME

I

J'ai voulu à ma détresse
des rues étroites, la caresse
à mes epaules des bons murs durs.
Mais vous les avez, ô hommes
élargis de vos pas,
de vos désirs,
de relents de rhum,
de sexe et de "draught-beer."
J'erre dans vos labyrinthes
multicolores et je suis las
de ma plainte.

II

Ainsi :
vers vous je suis venu
avec mon grand cœur nu
et rouge, et mes bras lourds
de brassées d'amour.
Et vos bras vers
moi se sont tendus très ouverts
et vos poings durs
durement ont frappé ma face.
Alors je vis :
vos basses grimaces
et vos yeux baveux
d'injures.

SONG OF MAN

I

I wanted for my anguish
narrow streets, the caress
on my shoulders of good hard walls.
But you have them, O men,
enlarged by your footsteps,
your desires,
stale smells of rum
sex and draught-beer.
I wander through your multicolored
labyrinths and grow weary
of my plaint.

II

And so:
to you I have come
with my great heart naked
and red, and my arms heavy
with armfuls of love.
And your arms were outstretched
wide open to me
and your hard fists
struck me hard in the face.
So then I saw:
your lowly grimaces
and your eyes slimy
with abuse.

Alors j'entendis
autour de moi coasser, pustuleux,
les crapauds — Ainsi :
Solitaire, sombre,
maintenant fort en mon ombre
mon seul compagnon fidèle,
je projette l'arc de mon bras
par-dessus le ciel.

Then I heard
around me croaking, pustulous
toads — And so:
Solitary, somber,
strong now in my shadow
my only faithful companion,
I cast the arc of my arms
across the sky.

.

ORAGE

Pour Ph. Thoby Marcelin

Le vent chassa un troupeau de bisons blanc dans la vaste prairie
du ciel. Silencieux et puissants ils écrasèrent
le soleil : le soleil s'éteignit
Le vent hurla telle une femme en mal
d'enfant :
La pluie accourut, fille du feu et de la mer ;
elle accourut en dansant
et tira sur le monde des rideaux de brume.
Les feuilles chantèrent
en tremblant comme des débutantes de music-hall ;
vint le tonnerre
et applaudit. Alors tout se tut pour laisser
applaudir le tonnerre ; des fleurs
moururent sans avoir vécu ; les palmiers agitèrent
leurs éventails contre la chaleur.
Un troupeau de bisons émigra de l'orient à
l'occident, et la nuit arriva comme une femme en deuil.

STORM

For Ph. Thoby Marcelin

The wind chased a herd of white buffalo across the vast prairie
of the sky. Silent and powerful they trampled on
the sun: the sun died out
The wind howled like a woman giving
birth:
The rain quickened, daughter of fire and the sea;
she quickened while dancing
and pulled curtains of mist over the world.
The leaves sang
while trembling like music-hall debutantes;
the thunder came
and clapped its hands. Then all fell silent to let
the thunder clap; the flowers died
without having lived; the palm trees shuddered
their palms against the heat.
A herd of buffalo emigrated from east to
west, and night came like a woman in mourning.

LANGSTON HUGHES

Tu connus à Lagos ces filles mélancoliques
Elles portent aux chevilles des colliers d'argent et s'offrent
nues
Comme la nuit encerclée de lune

Tu vis la France sans prononcer de paroles historiques
— Lafayette nous voici —
La Seine parut moins belle que le Congo

A Venise, tu cherchas l'ombre de Desdémone
Elle s'appelait Paola
Tu lui disais : Amorossissima
Et parfois
Babe, Baby
Alors elle pleurait et te réclamait vingt lires

Tu as promené ton cœur nomade, comme un Baedecker, de
Harlem à Dakar
La mer a prêté à tes chants un rythme doux et rauque, et
ses fleurs d'amertume écloses de l'écume.
Maintenant dans ce caberet où á l'aube tu murmures :
Jouez ce blues pou' moa
O jouez ce blues pou' moa
Rêves-tu de palmes et de chants de pagayeurs au crépuscule?

LANGSTON HUGHES

At Lagos you knew those melancholy girls
They adorn their ankles with silver bracelets and offer
themselves naked
As the night ringed by the moon

You saw France without pronouncing historic words:
> *Lafayette, we are here*
The Seine appeared less beautiful than the Congo

In Venice, you sought the shade of Desdemona
Her name was Paola
You said to her: *Amorossissima*
And sometimes
Babe, Baby
Then she wept and claimed her twenty lira from you

Your nomad heart wandered
like a Baedecker from Harlem to Dakar
The sea bestowed a sweet, rasping rhythm to your songs, and
its biting flowers opened in the salt spray.
Now in this cabaret at sunrise you murmur:
Play the blues for me
O play the blues for me
Do you dream of palm trees and negro paddlers singing
                                        down the dusk?

CRÉOLE

Sous la tonnelle,
L'as-tu rencontrée, sous la tonnelle
La négresse vêtue de blanches mousselines
— Viergine, je m'appelle
A votre service, monssié —

Au bord de l'eau,
L'as tu vue au bord de l'eau, sous les bougainvilliers
La négresse fraîche et nue comme l'ombre.

Viergine, Grâce
Vêtues de blanches mousselines ou d'ombre en fleur,
Mes rieuses négresses,
Combien vous sutes bénir ce cœur toujours inapaisé.

CREOLE

Under the leafy arbor,
Did you meet her, under the leafy arbor
The negress dressed in white muslin
My name is Viergine . . .
At your service, sir . . .

Beside the water,
Have you seen her beside the water, under the bougainvilleas
The negress fresh and naked as the shade.

Viergine, Grace
Dressed in white muslin or in budding shade,
My laughing negresses,
O you know how to bless this forever unappeased heart.

QUAND BAT LE TAM-TAM

Ton cœur tremble dans l'ombre, comme le reflet
        d'un visage dans l'onde troublée
L'ancien mirage se lève au creux de la nuit
Tu connais le doux sortilège du souvenir
Un fleuve t'emporte loin des berges,
Entends-tu ces voix : elles chantent l'amoureuse douleur
Et dans le morne, écoute ce tam-tam haleter telle la gorge
        d'une noire jeune fille.

Ton âme, c'est le reflet dans l'eau murmurante où
        tes pères ont penché leurs obscurs visages
Et le blanc qui te fit mulâtre, c'est ce peu
        d'écume rejeté, comme un crachat, sur le rivage.

WHEN THE TOM-TOM BEATS

Your heart trembles in the shadows, like the reflection
      of a face in troubled water
The old mirage rises from the hollow of the night
You know the sweet sorcery of memory
A river carries you far from the banks,
Do you hear those voices: they're singing love's heartache
And in the mournful darkness, hear that tom-tom panting
      like a young black girl's breasts.

Your soul is the reflection in the murmuring water where
      your ancestors bent their dark faces
And the white man who made you a mulatto is this bit of
      sea spume cast out, like spit, upon the shore.

GUINÉE

C'est le lent chemin de Guinée :
La mort t'y conduira.
Voici les branches, les arbres, la forêt,
Ecoute le bruit du vent dans les longs cheveux
d'éternelle nuit.
C'est le lent chemin de Guinée :
Tes pères t'attendent sans impatience
Sur la route : ils palabrent.
Ils t'attendent.
Voici où les ruisseaux grelottent
Comme des chapelets d'os.
C'est le lent chemin de Guinée :
Il ne te sera pas fait de lumineux accueil
Au noir pays des hommes noirs :
Sous un ciel fumeux, percé de cris d'oiseaux
Autour de l'œil du mangot
Les cils des arbres s'écartent sur la clarté

pourrissante
Là t'attendent au bord de l'eau un paisible village et
La case de tes pères et la dure pierre familiale
Où reposer ton front.

GUINEA

It is the slow road of Guinea:
Death will guide you there.
Here are branches, trees, the forest,
Listen to the sound of the wind through the long hair
of eternal night.
It is the slow road of Guinea:
Your forefathers are waiting for you patiently
On the road: they are chatting.
They wait for you.
Here is where the streams shake
Like bone rosaries.
It is the slow road of Guinea:
No bright reception will greet you
In the dark land of dark men:
Under a smokey sky pierced by cries of birds
Around the river's eye
The trees' eyelashes wander over the decaying

light
There, waiting for you beside the water, is a peaceful village
and the hut of your forefathers and the hard ancestral stone
Where your brow will rest forever.

MADRID

Cette ride sinistre de la sierra et l'horizon cerné d'un orage
　　　　　de fer
le ciel n'a plus un sourire plus un seul tesson d'azur pas un arc
　　　　　à lancer l'espoir d'une flèche de soleil
le arbres déchiquetés se redressent, gémissent comme des
　　　　　violons désaccordés
tout un village endormi dans la mort s'en va à la dérive
quand la mitrailleuse crible la passoire du silence
quand explose la cataracte de fracas
que le plâtras du ciel s'écroule

Et les flammes tordues lèchent dans la cité les blessures des
　　　　　lézardes calfatées de nuit
et dans le petit square abandonné où règne maintenant la paisible
épouvante il y a
mais oui il y a sur le visage sanglant de cet enfant un sourire
comme une grenade écrasée à coups de talon

Plus d'oiseaux de doux chants d'oiseaux de collines
l'âge de feu et d'acier est né la saison des sauterelles
　　　　　apocalyptiques
et les tanks avancent l'invasion obstinée de gros hannetons
　　　　　ravageurs
et l'homme est terré avec sa haine et sa joie pour demain
et quand il s'élance
la mort te vendange Hans Beimler
la mort qui agite sur le van de la plaine une moisson de cris

MADRID

This sinister ripple of the sierra and the horizon engulfed
        in an iron storm
the sky no longer has a smile no longer one azure patch not a
        bow to let loose hope on a sun-filled arrow
lacerated trees hold themselves erect, groaning like
        out-of-tune violins
an entire village in a dead sleep is cast adrift
when the machine gun riddles holes through the silence
when a roaring cataract explodes
and rubble falls from the sky

And in the city twisted flames lick the wounds of
        the cracks caulked with night
and in the small abandoned square where a peaceful terror
        now reigns there is
yes there's a smile on the bloody face of that child
like a pomegranate crushed under grinding heels

No more flying off with the sweet songbirds of the hills
the age of fire and steel is born the season of apocalyptic
        locusts
and tanks advance the undaunted invasion of ravaging
        June bugs
and man is buried with his hatred and his joy for tomorrow
and when he springs forth
death harvests you Hans Beimler
death which winnows a harvest of cries on the plains

Voici avec la neige la denture cariée des montagnes
l'essaim des balles bourdonnant sur la charogne de la terre
et la peur au fond des entonnoirs est comme le ver dans une
   pustule crevée

Qui se rappelle l'incroyable saison le miel des vergers
   et le sentier sous les branches
le murmure froissé des feuilles et le rire tendre et bon
   de la jeune femme
la part du ciel et le secret des eaux

— Il y a longtemps déjà que tomba dans l'oliveraie Lina Odena
là-bas dans le Sud.

C'est ici l'espace menacé du destin
la grève où accourue de l'Atlas et du Rhin
la vague confondue de la fraternité et du crime déferle
sur un espoir traqué des hommes,
mais c'est aussi malgré les sacrés-cœurs brodés sur l'étendard
   de Mahomet
les scapulaires les reliques
les gris-gris du lucre
les fétiches du meurtre
les totems de l'ignorance
tous les vêtements du mensonge les signes démentiels du passé
ici que l'aube s'arrache des lambeaux de la nuit
que dans l'atroce parturition et l'humble sang anonyme du
   paysan et de l'ouvrier
naît le monde où sera effacé du front des hommes la flétrissure
   amère de la seule égalité du désespoir.

Here with the snow the decayed teeth of the mountains
the swarm of bullets buzzing around the earth's carrion
and fear at the bottom of the bomb crater is like the worm
            inside an oozing sore

A reminder of the wonderful season the honey of orchards
            and the footpath under the branches
the crumpled murmur of leaves and the tender, innocent laughter
            of a young woman
the patch of sky and the water's secret

— It is already long ago that Lina Odena fell in the olive grove
down there in the South.

Here is space menaced by destiny
the shore where running from the Atlas Mountains and the Rhine
the confused wave of fraternity and crime breaks
on a hope sought after by men,
but also it is despite the sacred hearts embroidered on
            Muhammad's banner
the scapulars the relics
the amulets of profit
the fetishes of murder
the totems of ignorance
all the clothing of lies the demented signs of the past
here where dawn tears itself from the last shreds of night
where a world is born of the atrocious womb and the humble
            anonymous blood of the peasant and worker
where the bitter brand of despair borne equally by all
            will be erased from man's brow.

THE PREY AND THE DARKNESS

Four Stories

Translated by Ronald Sauer

Talk And Nothing More

The square was small and miserably lit by a single streetlamp. The crowd flowed past it from out a narrow alley, and starving dogs, being pursued, ran by and barked angrily.

But behind the mass of ramshackle houses, out there in the night, you could hear the sinister and joyous voice of a drum, the voice of a thousand African gods, mirthful and obscene, that punctured the silence with frenzied little beats.

"What made you say, Daniel, that they all look pathetic?"

Leaning back against a clear patch of wall, he turned toward the darkness that his question addressed.

From there came the response:

"Because it is all moving towards pleasure. Gaiety doesn't attract happiness. You seem to believe that I color everything with my own discouragement . . . Not really. We could move under that arbor and join their wholesale joy, dance with them and drink sweet rum. I would show you these men and women, show you their faces, and then you would realize that a happy crowd is composed of sad people. You'd see the hopelessness of their pleasure. But maybe you'd like to come back later, when it's all over. At a time when the crowd is gone, at a livid daybreak when there is nothing left but a mangy herd. At that hour when crowds dwindle like fruit dropping from their clusters. Each one of them bitter."

He grew silent. In the distance the drumbeat resounded like a pounding heart. Against the white wall flooded with light red flowers peculiar to the region exploded brilliantly.

The flowers diffused an acrid odor, fleshy and delicious; bleeding like a voluptuous wound, and their shadow, in splashes on the wall, seemed like a second bouquet, but of black roses, stained with the blood of others, in clots.

At that moment a song rose up in the night air, rose up in a slow rush, a moan from the depths, which became a piercing cry that leapt into the sky and then fell back to the earth again in sobs.

"Listen!" Daniel said, moving forward.

At which point the contours of his shoulders stood out.

"Listen. The voice of our race. All the sad pain of plantation-slaves living under the whip . . . "

Abruptly, without warning, he burst out laughing. The voice was white, it was trembling, then broke into a kind of rage.

"Let's go over there. Surely that's a beautiful, strong negress: her eyes half-shut, face brilliant with sweat beneath her calico scarf, singing the most awful of all possible songs, the obscene song, the mad call for oblivion, for total annihilation. I love prostitutes with their aching kisses, that ache from having bruised the flesh of their mouths against so many strange lips, in so many vile embraces. When I'm around them I feel at peace. I'm their equal. You don't believe it? You think I'm drunk, don't you? Perhaps. But that's not the reason, that—is—not—the—reason. Their equal in suffering, in day-to-day disgust. Prostituted myself: to myself, to my impotence, to my cowardice before life."

There followed a silence, battered by the drum.

"And also, you know, there's this dark flesh the color of soft, melting kiwi-fruit. And those enormous eyes, like bottomless wells, you might say. And hair 'like a herd of goats afloat on the mountainside of Gilead.' And what marvelous eyelids, covered with an ashen-mauve, from the ashes of their nights of love. Truthfully, very beautiful; and ideally, exquisitely stupid."

That cracked laugh possessed him again.

Jean interrupted him, placing a friendly and authoritative hand on his shoulder.

"Be quiet," he said. "You beat yourself up willingly, and that's a sign of weakness. I know the bitterness you live with, but — forgive the banality of this advice — you have to do something about it. You seem to take pleasure in letting yourself go."

He was mumbling because, loving Daniel as he did, he was sincerely moved by him.

Daniel made an almost brutal movement toward him with his shoulder, as if pushing through a narrow doorway:

"Go ahead. I know what you're going to tell me. That I have what it takes 'to succeed.' But what do you mean by 'succeed?' To be a lawyer, an engineer, a doctor, or worse, a politician; to make money in order to eat well, to have a car and be part of a circle of some kind. But such satisfactions are for unthinking animals. No, I'll never 'succeed.' Besides, you're forgetting that I'm black! Someday, at noon, go over to Grand Street and watch them go by in their luxurious cars, these mulattos, 'grand negroes,' melting in the heat of their fat, like chocolate in the sun; then you'll better understand the fable of the earthen and iron pots. But that good man La Fontaine simply did not know that in the one there is coffee and in the other cocoa.

"But don't misunderstand me. I bear no grudge against these people. I wouldn't lower myself. Besides, I have nothing against them in particular, but against the *environment* to which they belong. And that *environment* has its reasons. You know, Jean, in Haiti this is the way things are: as soon as a man tries to find his own way and leave the herd, he gets treated like a black sheep; as soon as a head rises above the level of the crowd, it is crushed. The *environment* fights back: an instinct for self-preservation, quite simply. Do you see what I mean?"

His voice was low and filled with anguish.

". . . Or maybe you find me ridiculously vain? Answer me: Is it all over for me, am I finished? Tell me, don't you think I might get myself out of this rut and change my life, live it as I've always dreamed it could be — great and beautiful? Ah! These doubts are killing me!"

His friend did not respond:

"Say something!" he demanded vehemently. "You too, you too believe that it's all over for me, that I'm a rotten tree trunk that the current washes downstream. You too condemn me."

"No, Daniel, but perhaps you're asking too much of life. The picture you paint of it is certainly noble; but isn't it unreal? And aren't you trying to attain the impossible?"

"You're trying to say that my desire is disproportionate to my strengths and that the imbalance that ensues can only amount to vain endeavors, only result in sterile convulsions. And again, one must know how to resign oneself, to bow down to some kind of paltry existence, to content oneself with little. Never. I refuse such a pitiful stoicism. No, say no more. Let it be. Forget the question altogether, shall we? Anyway, it doesn't matter."

Jean did not have the courage to protest. He felt powerless before the strength of Daniel's despair, and he felt ashamed.

They walked away from the deserted square and entered a labyrinth of narrow dark streets that were hemmed in by half-collapsed hovels smelling like a garbage dump, and got sidetracked down a cul-de-sac, but since Daniel knew the area well enough, they soon found their way out again, crossing some courtyards that were sound asleep, then they reemerged by the Produce Wharf.

The place presented its familiar face, gnawed into by the night, with the look of a filthy leper. Here and there, above the french fries and peas-and-rice stalls, glimmered the smoke-filled light of candles. The expanse of the sea was like a peaceful beast ruminating in a low and continuous rumbling. A cloying smell of rotting seaweed and fish wove itself into the odor of grease from the saucepans.

The drumbeat could now be heard as a mere distant stammering.

At that moment a stocky, short-legged man came toward them. He was waving a large slice of browned potato, as one would a welcoming handkerchief. From his solid round bull's head and high-spirited bearing they soon saw that it was none other than the poet Emilio.

Already, from a distance, they felt engaged by the sound of his voice, full, as it was, of commotion and leaps of brilliance.

"Hey! Noble loafers, what brings you here to this market of the night, so unlikely a place for the subtleties of metaphysical speculation."

"How's it going, Emilio?"

"Very badly, thank God."

He was laughing, and in order to shake the hands that Daniel and Jean were extending towards him, he held his golden potato in his teeth: he had the air of a negress holding a tray.

"You, Daniel, I know what brings you around here: I know about your spice-merchant's tastes for certain feminine perfumes: pepper, musk, incense and armpits. Ha, Haaa! . . . But you're probably hungry. Come on!"

And he led his unresisting companions through the whirlwind of his words and exuberance toward the place of a merchant-woman.

The woman was a layered mass of formless flesh. Her bust spilled over onto her stomach and her stomach over onto her rump.

This butterball was busy cooking when they arrived, and a white smile lit up the gleaming mole that was her face.

"Hénaurme, it's really you!" Emilio said with tenderness. "Allow me to introduce you: Madam Rose Roselis, my friends Daniel and Jean, the one a doctor, the other a lawyer. As you can see, outstanding representatives of the intellectual and social scenes. Nothing astonishing in that, now is there? All Haitians are lawyers or doctors. Nothing to it, it's in the blood: among the African tribes the con-artist and the witch doctor were very highly esteemed."

A lyrical sarcasm caused his demonic little eyes to narrow as his body swelled up in sweeping gestures.

"As for Madam Rose, this remarkable beauty, she is my muse. Take a good look at her, this daughter of the African Black Jupiter and some charming hippopotamus."

She was quietly heaping lard into a cauldron using a big wooden spoon.

"She inspires me, this woman, there's no doubt about it. For example, listen to this magnificent Alexandrine — destined to drive our Afro-Latino intellectuals — I was going to say our frightful Latinos — crazy, so beautifully rendered by Morand who writes of their lips more purple than grapes which only open to speak in the imperfect subjunctive:

> *Your ass is a voluptuous drumboat,*
> *delectably laden and a fitting feast.*

Your ass is: O sweet intimations! You can hear the first hiss of the grease slipping into the pan.

A voluptuous drumboat: like dreamboat, only with an explosive beat, and it makes one dream of a swaying behind, of a great pot blackened by a life in the fire.

Delectably laden: appetizing, to what the sluice gates of salivation, wherewith we are then carried away to the feast that awaits us!"

He was laughing full-throatedly and with such hearty good humor that everyone was infected with his gaiety. Even the impassive Rose herself was shaken by a fit of laughter and cackled like a mother hen.

"Tell me, Emilio," Daniel asked, getting serious again. "Why are you no longer writing? I mean how come you haven't published anything new?"

Emilio cracked a wry smile, you might have said that his laughter had taken refuge in the folds of his features, the lines of which suddenly pulled at his lips with a bitterness.

"I haven't published anything new because I haven't written anything new."

His wry smile now went much deeper.

"You ruined my evening. You make me come back to myself, as to an old abandoned road. For some time now I've been losing myself, running away; and now you stir up the dust of my rancor. Don't apologize, Daniel, we're old friends. You needn't apologize."

For a while he seemed to be reflecting.

"Poetry, poetry . . . One doesn't live by poetry; at least, not here in Haiti. Yet the work is there, ripened, grown large — but then it shrivels up. I like the way Goethe puts it: one writes a book to get it out of one's system, just as a tree produces its fruit. But I ask myself: how to get at it? Ah! To realize that a book, a poem, is so perfect, that in giving them birth one lightens one's own load, at the same time clearing a path that leads to greatness!"

Excuse me, Emilio," Daniel said in a stifled voice. "I thought you were happy."

"Happy? You'd thought so because I take to my life passionately, as one takes to a woman. But after making love, Daniel, as the eyes become clear again, there appears a sudden, terrible clarity . . . "

Jean interrupted.

"What is most wanting in the character of Haitian intelligence is a sense of commitment to discipline, of being focused on a goal, stubbornly. The most interesting energies are dissipated. But it requires superhuman resolve to persist in a chosen path, when the faith that guides you meets with no encouragement and only comes up against misunderstanding, that most treacherous form of passive resistance."

"And then," said Emilio, through clenched teeth, "where is one to find a discipline? In politics? In Haiti, nationalism is the subtotal of special interests that clash and repel one another.

"Let's not talk about marriage. I know many young girls who would make such charming mistresses, if only they weren't so empty-headed and honest."

Dawn was coming on. The night was slipping off like a mask and glimmerings of light reached up and into the sky, like pale fingers that left smudged traces above the gloom.

They felt full of sadness, forsaken and useless, like the smashed crates and shards of pottery that lay strewn about them all over the ground.

Jean was the first to go off.

Daniel took his companion's arm.

"Emilio, do you know this line from Leopardi: *Man would be all powerful, if he could live all his life in hopelessness . . .* ? Indeed, he would draw undreamed-of strength from the depths of himself, if his old sufferings were in no way a sullen habit. This is without doubt our very problem: our despair in the face of the poverty of our lives is now but a mere bad habit; it doesn't motivate us, it doesn't force our minds to leap: on the contrary, it's a heavy burden that weighs us down, bending us more and more towards the ground."

They walked over to the wharf.

The sea was composed of a million tiny, metallic reflections.

They stood there without saying anything else, listening to

the rustling silk of the waves lapping against the pilings.

At last, they went their separate ways, for a cold drizzle had begun to fall out of the pale morning sky.

The Jacket

When he came into the bar, Saivre felt like a sailor touching down on firm ground again.

The posters on the wall were glossy and shone through the dense cigarette smoke. He seated himself in a dark corner. A drunk was sleeping next to him. He shoved him aside, to make room for himself and get comfortable. The drunk half-opened his glassy eyes and said: "Napoleon died in his bed," and immediately went back to sleep. Saivre was not amused by the thought and he turned to look out the window. The rain caused the light from the streetlamp to dissolve. Fine, golden needles fell through its aura. Beyond it, the deep night, the vast black silence.

"If somebody left the door open," Saivre thought, "everyone in here would shut up. Silence would fill the room and take them by their throats."

He was feeling good, but the noise was making him feel sick. Voices rose up and broke against his forehead.

A prostitute climbed the stairs on the arm of a sailor. Her gestures were heavy with weariness. Saivre's thoughts followed her for a moment. He pictured her white, crucifying herself on a dirty red bedspread.

"Why red?" he wondered right away. He couldn't say. But he was certain the bedspread was red.

He had a glass of whiskey, then a second, and a third. Then he grew very warm, took off his jacket and hung it on a nail on the wall facing him.

A conversation rose up from the back of the room. A woman's voice climbed to a high pitch and then cleanly broke off. Then everything settled down to a confused murmur. The drunk woke up again. He had a drawn face and a drowned look. A little scar in the form of a V made for a curious tattoo on his forehead. Suddenly the spectacle of the man filled Saivre with a frightful disgust. He felt almost physically ill to realize how close to him he was and he shuddered violently to hear him say:

"Comrade, you'll have a drink with me?"

Saivre accepted nevertheless.

They drank after clicking glasses.

The drunk said to him:

"My name is Milon, and yours?"

"What's it to you?" Saivre grumbled back.

A silence followed, then Milon started in again.

"And business, how's business?"

"I don't do any business!" Saivre nearly shouted back.

An unexpected rage rose to his head and he leaned back a bit as if he might spring at him.

"Good. Good. That's fine," Milon said.

A heavy calm fell, settling between them.

A phonograph wept in the hoarse voice of an old female singer.

The sad, dumb and romantic lyrics of the song echoed off the narrow walls of the room. A woman was weeping softly in her folded arms. The men in the room fell silent and forgot their drinks.

Then Milon said:

"I see, like a hanged-man, you could say."

Saivre jumped:

"Huh? What d' ya mean? Where?"

"Oh, I was only joking," Milon said shyly, "but your jacket."

Saivre looked at his jacket with such painful attention that his eyes started to hurt. His jacket, a miserable thing, patched-up, threadbare, was hanging where he had left it.

And Milon's voice again:

"Wouldn't you say, wouldn't you say so?"

Saivre called to the waiter and ordered a bottle. He looked at it, and, one swig after another, downed two huge glassfuls. Then:

"Tell me, why did you say that?"

"Me? For no reason. Just an idea . . . "

"Come on, why did you say that," Saivre said through clenched teeth.

"I really don't know, to tell you the truth. Actually, it could be it made me think of the kid who hung himself last month at our place."

"Really?"

"Yes. A very young man who had lived for a long time overseas. He'd left his family. He and his father didn't get along. We took him in, my wife and I, as a boarder. He wrote poetry all day long, read a pile of books, and didn't pay up. A son-of-a-bitch, huh? One morning, he was found hanging there. He owed us for two month's worth. Never even mentioned it, the swine!"

"So?" Saivre asked.

He was deathly pale and his fingers fidgeted around his glass without being able to pick it up.

"Well! He looked just like your jacket. He was hanging there like a rag," Milon said, feeling more and more sure of himself now. "Just like it, just like it," he repeated.

"It isn't true," murmured Saivre, fixing his bulging eyes on the jacket.

"Yes. Just like it. Just like it."

"No. No."

"Yes. I can still see it clearly. Absolutely the same."

"Shut up, demon," said Saivre in a low voice.

"But I'm telling you. Ex-act-ly-like-your-jac-ket."

"Shut up, demon," Saivre said again in a voice so low that Milon hardly heard him.

He could not take his eyes off his jacket now. An insane anguish danced in his eyes.

Milon was silent. He drank in little gulps, smacking his tongue on his palette after each swallow. Time dragged on. The phonograph was silent. But a sailor, his arm around a woman's neck, was singing:

Somebody loves me . . .

Suddenly Saivre asked:

"Tell me, you, after one's kicked the bucket, right! What's your idea? Do you suppose, do you think there's . . . another life, or . . . ?"

Milon thought for a brief moment:

"No. I don't think so."

"Me neither," Saivre said with such effort that it twisted his whole face.

Painfully he got up and made for the door.

"Hey! Don't forget your jacket."

"No, no," Saivre groaned, and he fled out and into the night. He ran, despite his drunkenness. A dog ran after him a short way down a deserted street.

He no longer felt the rain. He didn't notice the houses going by. He didn't even see his own shadow.

He fled. Words were dancing about his head, kicking up an awful suffering:

"The jacket, the hanged man, the jacket, the hanged man."

48

He was muttering through his teeth:

"No. No. I don't want it anymore. It has to be done with."

At last, he arrived home. It was a miserable wooden shack. He simply pushed the door and it opened.

She, in bed, when she hears him coming, takes refuge against the wall.

"Oh God, Oh God," she thinks, "if only he doesn't hit me so hard today."

She waits for the blows, but they do not come.

She hears him light a candle, moving among the furniture. Disjointed words reach her ears: "The jacket. Ex-act-ly. Ah! the demon. Just like the jacket."

A chair fell over. Nothing more, nothing more than the anguish that glued her to the wall.

She said to herself:

"He's fallen asleep."

Still, she prudently waited. For how long? The day had not yet begun filtering through the poorly joined wooden boards.

At last, with infinite cautiousness, she turned over. By the light of the candle, she saw the hanging body. Then she let out a scream.

The neighbors came running . . .

Part Of A Confession

"Here I am more alone than the shadows of the room; the window lets only the night in, hardly scared off by the shy light of the lamp, about which it flutters like a dark butterfly.

"Here I am on my deserted island: this pale, flat rock of a table, completely surrounded by the eddying silence, the wash of shadows.

"This peaceful and indifferent hour. All noise tip-toes off and away, and the revery of half-closed eyes gently comes in.

"To try my hand one more time at the deceptive experience of looking into the past, as into a river swollen with the cries and rustling wings of these furtive seagulls: memories.

"Narcissus grown old, my face no longer speaks to me, with its deep wrinkles and valleys of lines, and its scars, conjoining a map too easily read, already stripped of its meager interest, neither beautiful nor ugly, simply marked by the experiences of a life of mediocrity.

"Mediocrity: I've already said the word, indicative of the painful fall of the sort of man who wavers on the wire stretched between desire and will. As far back as I can go with the recollections of youth, I come up against this image of a tight-rope walker with outstretched arms ever closing in on his goal, but then at the last moment he loses his balance, symbolic of my powerlessness *to realize* my life.

"And I ask myself, these days, if it wasn't my desire that was the insurmountable thing, the thing that drained me, for the greater it grew, the more it prevented any possible satisfaction, hence I've become incomplete and content with doing without.

"In my struggle with this shadow, all my life long, I was aloof. One consolation remained for me, a world that opened on subtle and comforting joys: with a burning passion I gave myself over to study. But I think this properly concerns the domain of great spirits, great souls, as part of their vast undertakings, where the idea, the profound thought, is inseminated.

"Insemination: sole promise of richness, kernel and future of progress. But in me all development shrivelled in the bud, each grain was neutralized and came to nothing. I was like a barren field, planted with saplings already in leaf that, instead of growing green and flourishing, just died off.

"Whereas I imagined I was the overseer of a body of knowledge, I was only a pedantic and sinister custodian, a caretaker of idea-corpses. And the books over which I leaned, as over a crib, to enjoy the first cry of a truth, remained for me the sarcophaguses covered with a black and glacial typographical dust.

52

"Here I am returned unto myself as from a very long journey. I had wandered among men and they were always foreign to me, for I thought that I was better than them, and I wanted to convince them of it. They repelled me into a bitter rancor and a despairing solitude. Hence I looked at them askance, with wary eyes and the snickering mouth of those unhappy types who lurk behind window curtains and spy on their neighbors in the sick hope of discovering something vile about them, the better to console themselves for their own pettiness. But I could not help looking at myself with pitiless clairvoyance, and my lips only bled with their own wounds.

"A friend? I knew nothing of the gentleness of a strong hand on my shoulder. It seems like the internal flame that animated me burned with an intensity to destroy my very life blood. And so I was like a tree, struck by lightning and thunderbolts, from which the birds had flown away.

"But I laughed to think that an outmoded *Weltschmerz* had gotten hold of me, although I constantly felt thrown back on myself and shut up in a circle of solitude. Indeed, I tried to integrate friendliness into my Self — Alas! There is no real friendliness, which is not conditioned by misunderstanding, and I looked back and down into myself with such sharp penetration that I could not, even in friendship, help but feel torn.

★ ★ ★

"Ah! Already the light trembles and quavers: an immeasurable shadow climbs up the wall, distends and then disappears. The brightness sheds its petals and dies. Nothing else beyond this silence except the vain dialogue of an old man complaining of himself to his cruel double.

"Silence, silence and its horribly anguished cry, stifled in a strangled throat! Ah! Would that this door open and a woman come in with tentative footsteps; would that she draw near to me with that mysterious smile I never knew, come right up to my forehead and useless arms and rekindle the lamp that has gone out, and she, the living light, that she in her warmth disperse this cold, spectral past which I have evoked. Yes, that I might, that I could live again in a present as fresh and new as spring: that I might feel against my cheeks the tender flower of her warm breasts unfold, that some sweet murmuring melt my solitude.

"Dear God, would that the door open and a very little child come in and climb right onto my lap, that I could hear his sweet little awkward voice say something, that he place his boyish hands on my old face. Dear God, could such a child love me?

"But, how well I know there is no one there; neither a woman to pity my beggarly distress, nor any child with fine, curly locks, nor a hoped-for friend to lighten my heart — like a fire asleep under unstirred ashes, unstirred by strong words as bright as morning.

"No, there is no one: the hour is unfavorable, except for some phantoms drifting up from oblivion. They drag me along with them, and I can not fend them off. "

★ ★ ★

Often, the dawn would creep up on Benoit Carrère, as he slept, his head there in his folded arms on the table, and the fans of the palm leaves would sprinkle fresh breezes upon his brow, but he would not wake up to them, no, he would not wake up.

★ ★ ★

54

The Making Of A Bureaucrat

Michael Rey, as he woke up, saw a dirty day slipping through the Venetian blinds. He smiled that smile peculiar to him: a kind of pained grin that pulled on his lips on the one side of his mouth where it was then concentrated into two divergent lines, and as was his habit, he soon asked himself why on earth was he smiling at this dull light, at the pretentious furnishings of this poorly appointed room that his wife was so proud of, and where floated and mingled the sweet odor of strong perfume and the bitter smell of his rubber raincoat, still wet with the downpour that had caught him by surprise coming home in the early hours of the morning, and on which little droplets of condensed water were still beading.

Seeing what remained of a puddle that was making a dark stain on the floorboards, Michael smiled again. This time he knew why.

It was five years ago . . . he was remembering the day he returned to Haiti. The midday sun tamed a silent sea gently moving with foamless waves. A profound joy took hold of him. In the anonymous shoving and pushing of the crowd, climbing onto the narrow gangway amid visitors, porters, and relatives, he saw himself at last, felt the joyous echo of this black world inside himself, felt Europe's iciness that had stuck to him melt, felt what he bitterly called "the great white silence" vanish, the racial abyss he'd left back there, which his friendships, his loves, and his relations could not ameliorate. Now he was among his brothers again. His people. He could have fallen to his knees and kissed the sweet Haitian earth.

Suddenly, the port danced before his eyes that were clouding over with tears.

While his parents shuffled him off toward town, they were relentlessly burdening him with a thousand questions. He attempted to answer them, but he just wanted to get away from them, to be alone and simply talk in solemn ecstasy, or embrace that woman selling her mangos, passing by with the basket of fruit on her head, with a dignity befitting a queen and her crown, her back arched, sure-footed, the great purple grapes of her ripe breasts bursting through the blue fabric of her blousy dress, yes, to hug her to me with all my strength and say: "Sister!" Or to take in my arms that ragged child with his hands imploring an American tourist, to press him against my breast and say: "Brother, little brother!"

. . . A clock rang out the hour. Michael fell back into the present. It was probably very late, since he couldn't hear his wife about. He got up wearily and began to get dressed, and again dreaming of his past, he resumed: "I've embraced life too vigorously, too forcefully. I've seized it by the throat, suffocated it . . . "

Just as he was finishing getting dressed, someone knocked at the door. The servant came in, bare-footed, her eyes lowered, with that air of wisdom characteristic of maids who make four o'clock mass, and she announced that Madam Ballin was waiting downstairs. Indeed.

Madam Ballin, widower, is Michael's mother-in-law. He despises this grotesque woman who embodies a yellow fleshiness the color of rotten mangos, in funereal dresses that gigantic cameos do nothing to enliven. Her small bony head, monstrously disproportionate to her enormous body, was so misshapen that it occurred to him it was structured for but one purpose: to offset the lower half of her face where a gaping, thin-lipped gorge of a mouth busied itself mincing up words like a meat cleaver. The whole effect filled him with such disgust as Madam Ballin could scarce comprehend. And she is proud of her pointed head; when she alludes to it her vain and comical manner says: "I have transcended the atavistic," meaning that her features retain nothing of their African origins. She is very much the daughter of Madam Ochsle, that mulatto woman who, having married a Teuton of sorry origin, but who, however, made a fortune within just a few years, referred to herself strictly in these terms: "Especially we German women!"

Michael hates her thoroughly and at the same time somehow loves her. He could not do without her. She is the object of his vengeance on Port-au-Prince society — corrupt, hypocritical, crassly bourgeois — which broke him, and which she epitomizes to perfection. He gets a real thrill from making her suffer, from hurting her, and he always succeeds, and with ease, for Madam Ballin is thoroughly superficial and practically asks for it.

He knows that his remarks will be repeated in the fashionable circles where, seated side by side, stiff in their 1880s corsets and overwhelmed by their bilious conditions, these women of the best neighborhoods spend their time deciding the happiness of newlyweds or meddle in the reputations of honest men.

And to think that his sarcasm shall not go unnoticed, indeed, will be communicated far and wide by this stupefying process that Haitians call "telemouth." Well, all this he finds gratifying and it fills him with contentment.

The hatred of Michael Rey for his mother-in-law is perhaps the only emotion he experiences powerfully enough to render his life tolerable. He clings to it the way a drowning man clings to a piece of flotsam, and if, perchance, he finds himself thinking that one day she will die, he doubtless realizes that he shall weep at her funeral.

Michael goes down to the livingroom without putting on a

jacket and with his feet buried in his big old slippers. One day his mother-in-law had said to him: "My dear son-in-law, an appearance *in shirtsleeves* is not very aesthetic. (She adores words that end in *ic* and *ism*, and albeit she does not fully understand them, she finds them very distinguished somehow.) He knows full well that this will infuriate her.

He delights in it, for there is something puerile about him that is not so much an index of lively emotion, as much as what remains of a childhood wholly without candor.

At bottom, he is rather like one of those mistreated, battered children whose mischievousness has something almost innocent about it, but who only take pleasure in devilish practical jokes in which their bitterness can find food for thought.

Madam Ballin spills over the sides of her chair and has resituated her eyeglasses on her large, low forehead. Michael has bid her a good day and listens to her talk on and on about meaningless things and examines her attentively. He can feel that she is winding up for a venomous phrase, wound up onto herself like the coils of a fat, four-eyed serpent about to spring.

"Jeanne isn't here?"

"No."

"You don't seem to be in such a good mood. You're working hard, I gather. That's what I hear everyone say, at least."

"Good God, if everyone says so, I have no reason to doubt it."

"Yes, Everyone's expecting your new book to come out. It seems that it will be a masterpiece. You're so good at gathering first hand information."

Michael did not respond.

"You're quite the worldly one since, under the pretext of studying the soul of the Haitian people, you've taken to frequenting those dives."

Madam Ballin's visits with Michael did not last very long. It would appear that the grotesque woman feels a desire to come see Michael, time and again, for the sole purpose of having words thrown in her face, which hurts her, and which circumstance, none-theless, she actually provokes.

"You deceive yourself, that's not my motivation. I go to them only after having attended a reception at the home of Mr. and Mrs. Coulette, crême-de-la-crême of Port-au-Prince. The frank debauch-ery of the one social life consoles and revives me from the hypo-critical caddiness of the other."

"My son-in-law, I will not permit you to speak . . . "

"Give me some peace," Michael interrupted her with unruffled aplomb. "You disgust me! All of you! I know what you keep hidden behind your beautiful appearances, your aristocratic airs, etc., etc., with your luxurious gown covering the sick prostitute's flesh. I'm telling you once more that I'm fed up with you and your life. Your whirlwind of worldliness doesn't tempt me at all. I've no interest in taking a spin in the void."

"Ah! It's easy to guess in what kind of company you've picked up these ideas. To think I've given my daughter to such a man!"

"Perhaps you would have done better to marry her off to one of those interesting gentlemen of the sensible-wisdom-type, cozy in their shelter of excess, a regular safety-valve and guaranteed Imposter-Brand, whom I've had the dubious honor of remarking at times in your drawingroom, taking a generous interest in chari-table works and the general progress of humanity, their hands in-terlocked on their thighs in touching gestures that allow one to foresee that later, once they've become Division Heads or sit on Boards of Directors, they'll only have to lean forward and round out their arms in order to twiddle their thumbs on virtuous pot-bellies adorned with gold chains and charms. My dear Mrs. Widow Ballin, how could you have not chosen for your Jeanne this high ideal of the mothers of Haitian families!"

"They're a thousand times better than you!" Madam Ballin cried out loud.

Her face, green with anger, was sweating an oil that refused to roll! Michael was looking at her with curiosity and asked himself how such a parched face could exude so much sweaty fat. He replied very calmly: "Well, then they couldn't be worth much," and he got up and walked out of the room, happy to have provoked such rage in her.

Beside herself, his mother-in-law howls: "You have no respect at all, you are wicked!"

Then louder, prophetically:

"You will go to hell!"

"Ha! Haaaaa! What bullshit!" Michael replies good naturedly, heading back upstairs to his room.

But once there, he regrets having left so soon, thinking of other insulting things he might have said to her, and he consoles himself, deciding that the very next day he will go to the "Everything's On Sale," where his aristocratic mother-in-law maintains a fairly lively hardware business.

II

He knots his tie, leaning into his reflection in the window. At the lower extreme of this Villa Bolosse just beyond the bouquets of palmtrees, like feather dusters dusting the sands pocked with raindrops, the sea stretches out with a grayness that could be called filthy, the color of corrugated sheetmetal.

It has been quite some time since this vision of the sea was able to move him at all. He looks out at the sea now with the eyes of a fisherman mourning the loss of his lines and tackle. Something deep inside him has clearly died. And how is one to be game for fishing without that rare bait: enthusiasm?

Michael Rey finds himself thinking that from now on his life shall unfold like this sea, with its to-and-fro motion, bitter and monotonous, without beautiful storms; and he is fully immersed in it and has not the strength to swim back to the surface. His descent will continue, slowly, until that day when, deep in the hole he has dug for himself, he shall no longer be moved by humanity's waves.

To kill time while waiting for this final appeasement, he can still insult his mother-in-law, still make his wife miserable and still drink countless cocktails of all shades and hues.

"And so to go on with this captivating day," he sighed, heading for the house of Horatio Basile, intending to partake of an aperitif.

The individual to whom this Shakespearean name applies is a "son of a good family," back in Haiti for several months now, after a sojourn in France, where he had gone to study law. With five thousand francs a month to spend, it is easy to fail one's exams. Horatio Basile flunked the first round, and as he was very persevering, he flunked the second, too. Breville Basile, a fat speculator in coffee and a man of practical sensibilities, immediately sent his son a check bereft of zeros and summarily ordered him to take the first boat back. Horatio, with much pain, tore himself from the arms of his lover and embarked (like a good Haitian) with several tailored suits and a very suggestive negligee by way of a keepsake. But he had not yet reached the Azores when Mr. Basile Sr., with a spontaneity that everyone had thought him incapable of displaying, suddenly died, leaving his son some thirty houses and two hundred and twenty-five thousand dollars made in commodities trade and custom duties from the port of Petit-Goave.

Several vast properties planted with coffee that he is in the process of liquidating keep him in Haiti — far from the Place Pigalle — here under our tropical sky, where he conducts an idle, scandalous, and noble life.

Physically, he very much resembles that type of street-artist whom the Haitians refer to as "scarcely mulatto": tall, skinny, with a tapering face the color of our red-clay waterjugs, and someone you always seem to see in profile, dominated by a short forehead whose frizzy, reddish-brown hair is untameable; with a neck like a bottle's, where, similar to mercury in a thermometer, there ceaselessly rises and falls a pointed and voluminous Adam's Apple, while his awkward, oversized and hesitant feet are always out of sync with his jerky arms, making one think of some huge crustacean.

He has three great passions: cars, phonographs, and Michael, whom he'd wanted to meet after reading his manifesto in the literary review "The Murdered Crocodile": *Lamartine, Crocodile Poetry and the New Afro-Haitian Literature.*

Michael was highly amused by their first meeting, during the course of which Horatio had said to him:

"I understand you perfectly, Mr. Rey. We have to destroy our weeping-willows, our coconut trees; from now on it is necessary to carry these landscapes within ourselves, isn't it so? Palmtrees, for example, should no longer be taken for granted as indigenous, but we ought to plant them, if I dare say so, in our very souls."

"Absolutely," Michael had replied with dead seriousness. "But we mustn't forget the black drum that is made here, made, as you well know, from an ass' hide."

Then, having joined forces with the heir to Breville Basile's fortune, each afternoon he'd drop by his place for cocktails and, come the end of each month, talk him out of some fairly significant sums of money.

III

"Hello Horatio!"

"Ciao!"

When Michael came in, Horatio was dancing amidst the full bar stacked with bottles and cocktail shakers, an immense couch, and nine phonographs of various makes arranged according to size in a pyramid-shaped hierarchy not unlike those of family photographs.

He was already very drunk. His nose reflected the lights around him. There was also a light in his eyes, but it burned with an un-certain intensity, which the alcohol would soon extinguish.

All of the phonographs were playing at once: grinding away at the black coffee bean of the blues.

Michael went from one to the next, with the abrupt gestures of a father distributing boxed-ears to his kids, and shut them all off. They remained silent, like good little children.

"Idiot," he said, pouring himself a manhattan, and he smiled with scorn.

Horatio attempted to focus his eyes upon a confused and shaky world in which only Michael appeared steady and upright, making himself another drink amidst this latest miracle, the multiplication of phonographs. He was having a hard time ungluing his tongue. Finally, with a stupefying English accent he said:

"Wwhhyyy?"

Michael was drinking with his eyes half-closed, and with each mouthful a spider leapt forward in his brain, pulling on the unrav-eled filaments of his thoughts.

Downing his fourth manhattan, he speaks:

"You've never seen a peasant woman coming down the hill-sides, winding along the wine-red path and around the knolls. She passes in between the banana tree, uprooted by the wind and lean-ing over, the mango-trees heavy with the honey of their fruits, the baobabs from whose branches hang scarves of parasites, the sacred mapous with their tentacle-like roots; she passes along on such graceful feet you'd take her for a dancer, the high bust and balanc-ing arms that make her large hips surge in *dolce armonioso*. At times her calloused feet hit a stone and set it rolling down the slope, leaping *decrescendo*. Ah! Music!

"I once saw a man in the doorway of his house beating his woman with a stick, and keeping time as he went about it, as if she were a tom-tom, and the poor creature submitted to the rhythm of it all, taking the blows upon her shoulders, while dancing and screaming and singing her pain.

"In Amsterdam I saw two black acrobats, naked animals in effect, swinging from a trapeze, entwined like a sixteenth note. The music was wholly superfluous, for they already were — bodies wet with sweat, legs nervous, and firm arms charged with bulging muscles — a magnificent, insolent hymn to life."

What buzzing bee was this that zig-zagged through the fallen silence? Horatio was stretched out on the couch, asleep, his legs spread eagle, his wet lips opening and closing again, sending forth the buzzing of a full-bodied snore.

I V

Jeanne was waiting for him in their modest drawingroom. He looks into her shadowy, sad eyes:

"Mother told me what you . . . Oh! Michael, why?"

She is plaintive and sweet against his body. He strokes her hair. Would she understand, if I told her, this horrible self-hatred that compels me to strike out at those I love?

"Oh! Michael, Michael, how unhappy you are!"

He rocks her:

"My dear, sweet little . . . "

"Michael, listen . . . "

He appeased her with a kiss. His two children, seated on a weaver's straw mat, amused themselves cutting out pictures from a department store catalog. They did not have his looks. How very strange they were to him! When he wanted to take them in his arms, they would cry.

And so his prison: this house of sadness. And the bars of his jail: a wife who doesn't understand him, and children who fear him and do not love him.

His whole future rises up before him like one long, tightly defined horizon, behind which life lives, powerful and beautiful, finely situated, and beyond his grasp.

Ah! Is it possible that this could be his irremediable fate, to be this man who is growing gray, broken in body and in soul, seated in an ugly room in a paltry house as a souptureen smokes beside him, with a wife grown old and fat?

A snickering mockery tears at him from within:

His entire future: waiting for rheumatism!

Now it is she who comforts him with a warm, rocking motion.

He leans on her shoulder, almost conquered, and already a spineless persuasion is creeping over him.

He abandons himself to the cowardly voice that says within him: give in, just give in. Flow with the warm stream. The victorious stand alone, they who know this: to have the cold, insensible patience of the shipwrecked. Have no fear of running aground, for it will be right there beside a normal happiness. And besides, aren't you ridiculous, pretending to cast your feeble fire into the infinite seas of life. Truly, you make me think of the madman who attempted to set fire to the sea with a match. And then, who are you to want to be a hero? Cast a glance behind you, and disgust will engulf your little heart. Once you took an interest in politics, you were never anything but a puerile pedagogue. You thought of yourself as a writer (you still do), you wrote manifestos, poems, and a book that no one read. You're just a pitiful bourgeois aware of your own ugliness, your impotence. This clear picture of yourself is your only real virtue. The day that your peers shall awaken from blindness, they will all rise up against one another and make a spectacle of themselves: a great pack of arrogant and embittered malcontents, all of them so certain that they're unrecognized geniuses.

Come on, get hold of yourself: you're thought of as the kind of guy who has what it takes to succeed: a good family, no rent to pay, and a place waiting for you in the Department of Interior. Take the job: one hundred and twenty-five dollars a month, your debts paid, the cloud hanging over you finally gone, your children will be happy, you'll be in touch with your relatives, reconciled with your family, it means happiness, life opening up for you.

You have struggled. You have used your will. You can't do it anymore. What good is fighting a battle that you already know you're going to lose?

And then his wife says:

"Listen, Michael, I've been to see mother. She told me that she talked with Pralier, you remember Pralier, the one so close to the Minister. The Minister came right out and said: 'Tell Madam Ballin that we are altogether disposed towards her son-in-law. He should write us a letter concerning the position.' Michael, think of your wife, your children, our poverty. (*And with a flash of revolt*) Everyone of my friends dresses better than me! Michael, accept the job, it will cost you so little; deep down you'll be just as free as before, and there's nothing to prevent you from thinking as you please. Just think, I'm still young, I love life, but I live like a hermit, a poverty case. I beg you, I implore you, accept."

She says it, she repeats it. Meanwhile he sinks into a quicksand of weariness.

For God's sake, she should shut up. He is lost, it is true, and broken, but would to God that this woman not barter his soul for her happiness.

He talks backs to her, gets up . . .

"Michael! . . ."

"Hold your tongue!"

But his voice is without fire. The pain that hollows out his features, that opens up depths of despair, is there in his eyes.

He goes off, ridiculously upright, like a drunk attempting to walk a straight line.

V

A poor little desk greets his distress. Here are his books, his last friends, but these too he has forsaken, and they are covered with dust that drifts up and plays in the sun's golden rays.

Here too are the reems of white paper piled on the table, and others covered with his writings, yellowed by time, the ink already fading.

His whole unlived life there before him.

His head in his hands, he reviews it:

"Am I limited by my own weakness, or is it indeed an inhuman desire which surpasses the bounds of an aspiration that I will not, that I can not propose for myself, it being beyond me!?!

"When we come right down to it, deep down, quite possibly it's just sour grapes, and I flatter myself with this disdain, when in reality I am incapable of the leap that would place my aspirations within reach.

"The whole thing is quite simple: I'm a failure, with clenched teeth, my life being a bunch of sour grapes that I can't even bite into.

"And what good is this pitiful soul searching? Each cross-examination that life is subjected to still leaves one with the question: Why? And each truth, painfully achieved, absurdly contains its own simple explanation.

"Or to put it another way, it repeats the same question:

"To what end? And more precisely: What good is it? *It* not being a question, but a retort. Indeed.

"Besides, is not this very analysis the proof, the best proof, of my weakness, my nothingness? The conceited flunky, endlessly ferreting in the void of himself, possessed by the fierce, wild hope (wild, even cruel, as he knows the hope to be vain) of discovering himself filled with unacknowledged virtues. I believe Carlyle when he says that the strong man, who knows what little there is to be known of himself, ought not to torment himself with questions, but set himself a task, and then: 'What you can do, do with Herculean resolve.' Alas! I've never had such pride. My vanity was all . . . only my self-embittered doubts, a bile I've heaped on others."

At such moments of complete and painful sincerity, Michael would feel relieved and freer, but this deliverance was short-lived, and in anguish he would soon feel the penetration of the old poison again, feel it take hold of him, suffocating him as he lives and breathes: he was like a vase that would empty itself only to be refilled with a new anguish.

He remained still, his forehead heavy in the palms of his hands.

"Ah! To put an end to all of that, to be finished with it."

He opened a drawer. The pistol was pointing toward him. He observed its black and shiny muzzle.

"One movement. I place the gun at my temple, a simple application of digital pressure and I've put a final red period at the end of the sentence of my life and its miseries."

But he felt himself to be a coward.

He did not close the drawer, but grabbing a sheet of white paper, he slowly, heavily, began:

To His Honor the Secretary of State,
It is my good fortune . . .

EBONY WOOD

BOIS D'ÉBÈNE

À Francine Bradley

PRELUDE

Si l'été est pluvieux et morne
si le ciel voile l'étang d'une paupière de nuage
si la palme se dénoue en haillons
si les arbres sont d'orgueil et noirs dans le vent et la brume

si le vent rabat vers la savane un lambeau de chant funèbre
si l'ombre s'accroupit autour du foyer éteint

si une voilure d'ailes sauvages emporte l'île vers les naufrages
si le crépuscule noie l'envol déchiré d'un dernier mouchoir
et si le cri blesse l'oiseau
tu partiras
abandonnant ton village

sa lagune et ses raisiniers amers
la trace de tes pas dans ses sables
le reflet d'un songe au fond du puits
et la vieille tour attachée au tournant du chemin
comme un chien fidèle au bout de sa laisse
et qui aboie dans le soir
un appel fêlé dans les herbages . . .

EBONY WOOD

To Francine Bradley

PRELUDE

If the summer is rainy and dreary
if the sky veils the pond with a cloudy eyelid
if the palm tree unravels into shreds
if the trees are arrogant and black in the wind and fog

If the wind blows a shroud of funeral dirge to the savanna
if the shadow crouches around a dying hearth

If a sail of ruthless wings carries the island toward shipwrecks
if the twilight drowns the torn flight of a last handkerchief
and if the cry wounds the bird
you will leave
abandoning your village

Its lagoon and bitter grapevines
the trace of your footsteps in its sand
a dream's reflection at the bottom of the well
and the old tower at the turn in the road
like a faithful dog at the end of its leash
and that howls in the night
a cracked call across the pastures . . .

Nègre colporteur de révolte
tu connais tous les chemins du monde
depuis que tu fus vendu en Guinée
une lumière chavirée t'appelle
une pirogue livide
échouée dans la suie d'un ciel de faubourg

Cheminées d'usines
palmistes décapités d'un feuillage de fumée
délivrent une signature véhémente

La sirène ouvre ses vannes
du pressoir des fonderies coule un vin de haine
une houle d'épaules l'écume des cris
et se répand par les ruelles
et fermente en silence
dans les taudis cuves d'émeute

Voici pour ta voix un écho de chair et sang
noir messager d'espoir
car tu connais tous les chants du monde
depuis ceux des chantiers immémoriaux du Nil.

Tu te souviens de chaque mot le poids des pierres d'Égypte
et l'élan de ta misère a dressé les colonnes des temples
Comme un sanglot de sève la tige des roseaux

Cortège titubant ivre de mirages
Sur la piste des caravanes d'esclaves
élèvent
maigres branchages d'ombres enchaînés de soleil
des bras implorants vers nos dieux

Negro peddler of rebellion
you know all the routes of the world
since you were sold in Guinea
a capsized light calls to you
a ghostly canoe
run aground on the soot of a suburban sky

Factory chimneys
decapitated palm trees with smoke-filled leaves
issuing a vehement signature

The siren opens its flood-gates
and from the presshouse of foundries flows
a wine of hatred a surge of shoulders a foam of cries
it spills into the alleys
ferments in silence
in the slum cauldrons of riots

Here for your voice is an echo of flesh and blood
black messenger of hope
for you know all the songs of the world
ever since those of the Nile's immemorial workpits.

Each word reminds you of the weight of Egyptian stones
and the muscle of your misery erected columns of temples
The way a sob of sap raises the stalks of reeds

Staggering procession drunk on mirages
On the trail of slave caravans
raising up
thin branches of shadows shackled against the sun
of arms imploring our gods

Mandingues Arada Bambara Ibo
gémissant un chant qu'étranglaient les carcans
(et quand nous arrivâmes à la côte

Mandingues Bambara Ibo
quand nous arrivâmes à la côte
Bambara Ibo
il ne restait de nous
Bambara Ibo
qu'une poignée de grains épars
dans la main du semeur de mort)
ce même chant repris aujourd'hui au Congo
mais quand donc ô mon peuple
les hivées en flamme dispersant un orage
d'oiseaux de cendre
reconnaitrai-je la révolte de tes mains?
et que j'écoutai aux Antilles
car ce chant négresse

qui t'enseigna négresse ce chant d'immense
peine
négresse des Iles négresse des plantations
cette plainte désolée

Comme dans la conque le souffle oppressé des mers

Mais je sais aussi un silence
un silence de vingt-cinq mille cadavres nègres
de vingt-cinq mille traverses de Bois-d'Ebène

Mandingo Arada Bambara Ibo
wailing a song strangled by iron collars
(and when we reached the coast

Mandingo Bambara Ibo
when we reached the coast
Bambara Ibo
there remained of us
Bambara Ibo
only a fistful of scattered grains
in the hand of the sower of death)
this same song taken up again today in the Congo
but when then O my people —
winter's winds in flames spreading a storm
of flying ashes —
will I recognize the rebellion of your hands?
and that I heard in the Antilles
for this song, negress,

who taught you, negress, this song of boundless
affliction
negress of the Islands negress of the plantations
this grieving moaning

Like the oppressed breath of the sea in a conch shell

But I also know a silence
a silence of twenty-five thousand negro corpses
twenty-five thousand railroad ties of Ebony Wood

Sur les rails du Congo-Océan
mais je sais
des suaires de silence aux branches des cyprès
des pétales de noirs caillots aux ronces
de ce bois où fut lynché mon frère de Géorgie
et berger d'Abyssinie

quelle épouvante te fit berger d'Abyssinie
ce masque de silence minéral

quelle rosée infâme de tes brebis un troupeau de marbre
dans les pâturages de la mort

Non il n'est de cangue ni de lierre pour l'étouffer
de geôle de tombeau pour l'enfermer
d'éloquence pour le travestir des verroteries du mensonge
le silence
plus déchirant qu'un simoun de sagaies
plus rugissant qu'un cyclone de fauves
et qui hurle
s'élève
appelle
vengeance et châtiment
un raz de marée de pus et de lave
sur la félonie du monde
et le tympan du ciel crevé sous le poing
de la justice

Afrique j'ai gardé ta mémoire Afrique
tu es en moi

Under the iron rails of the Congo-Océan
but I know
the shrouds of silence in the cypress branches
the petals of black bloodclots on the brambles
in that woods where they lynched my brother of Georgia
and, shepherd of Abyssinia,

what terror made you, shepherd of Abyssinia,
this iron mask of silence

what vile dew turned your sheep into a marble flock
in the pastures of death

No there is neither pillory nor ivy to choke it
no prison no tomb to imprison it
no eloquence to disguise the pettiness of lies
silence
more destructive than a simoon of assegais
more howling than a cyclone of savage beasts
and which roars
rears up
summons
vengeance and punishment
a tidal wave of puss and lava
on the world's felony
and the sky's eardrum shattered under the fist
of justice

Africa I kept your memory Africa
you are in me

Comme l'écharde dans la blessure
Comme un fétiche tutélaire au centre du village
fais de moi la pierre de ta fronde
de ma bouche les lèvres de ta plaie
de mes genoux les colonnes brisées de ton abaissement . . .

POURTANT

Je ne veux être que de votre race
ouvriers paysans de tous les pays
ce qui nous sépare
les climats l'étendue l'espace
les mers
un peu de mousse voiliers dans un baquet d'indigo
une lessive de nuages séchant sur l'horizon
ici des chaumes un impur marigot
là des steppes tondues aux ciseaux de gel

Des alpages
la rêverie d'une prairie bercée de peupliers
le collier d'une rivière à la gorge d'une colline
le pouls des fabriques martelant la fièvre des étés

D'autres plages d'autres jungles
l'assemblée des montagnes
habitée de la haute pensée des éperviers
d'autres villages
est-ce tout cela climat étendue espace
qui crée le clan la tribu la nation
la peau la race et les dieux
notre dissemblance inexorable?

Like a splinter in the wound
Like a guardian fetish in the village center
make of me your catapult stone
of my mouth the lips of your wound
of my knees the broken columns of your abasement . . .

BUT

I only want to be of your race
workers peasants of all countries
that which separates us
climate distance space
the oceans
a bit of foam sailboats in a bucket of indigo
clouds hanging out to dry on the horizon
here, fields of stubble the adulterated stream
there, the steppes sheared by scissors of frost

The mountain grasslands
the reverie of a meadow lulled by rocking poplars
a river necklace around the throat of a hill
the pulse of factories hammering out summer's fever

Other beaches other jungles
the assembly of mountains
inhabited by the lofty thought of the sparrow hawk
other villages
is all that climate distance space
what creates the clan the tribe the nation
the skin the race and the gods
our inexorable unlikeness?

Et la mine
et l'usine
les moissons arrachées à notre faim
notre commune indignité
notre servage sous tous les cieux invariable?

Mineur des Asturies mineur nègre de Johannesburg métallo
de Krupp dur paysan de Castille vigneron de Sicile paria
des Indes

    (je franchis ton seuil — réprouvé
    je prends ta main dans ma main — intouchable)

garde rouge de la Chine soviétique ouvrier allemand de la
prison de Moabit indio des Amériques
Nous rebâtirons
Copen
Palenque
et les Tiahuanacos socialistes
Ouvrier blanc de Détroit péon noir d'Alabama
peuple innombrable des galères capitalistes
le destin nous dresse épaule contre épaule
et reniant l'antique maléfice des tabous du sang
nous foulons les décombres de nos solitudes

Si le torrent est frontière
nous arracherons au ravin sa chevelure
intarissable
si la sierra est frontière
nous briserons la mâchoire des volcans
affirmant les cordillères

And the mine
and the factory
the harvests torn from our hunger
our common indignity
our servitude under every unchanging sky?

Miner of Asturias negro miner of Johannesburg
Krupp steelworker hardened Castilian peasant Sicilian
winegrower pariah of the Indies

    (I cross your threshold — an outcast
    I take your hand in mine — an untouchable)

Red Guard of China Soviet citizen German worker
of Moabite prison Indian of the Americas
we will rebuild
Copan
Palenque
and, socialists of Tiahuanaco,
white worker of Detroit black sharecropper of Alabama
countless multitudes of capitalist galleys
destiny unites us shoulder to shoulder
and repudiating the ancient malefice of blood taboos
we trample down the ruins of our solitude

If the mountain stream is a border
we will tear from the ravine its inexhaustible
hair
if the sierra is a border
we will shatter the jaw of volcanoes
affirming the sweep of the cordilleras

et la plaine sera l'esplanade d'aurore
où rassembler nos forces écartelées
par la ruse de nos maîtres

Comme la contradiction des traits
se résout en l'harmonie du visage
nous proclamons l'unité de la souffrance
et de la révolte
de tous les peuples sur toute la surface de la terre

et nous brassons le mortier des temps fraternels
dans la poussière des idoles

Bruxelles, juin 1939

and the plains will be the esplanade of dawn
where to reassemble our forces divided
by the cunning of our masters

As the contradiction of features
is resolved into the harmony of the face
so we proclaim the unity of suffering
and of revolt
of all the peoples on the surface of the earth

and we mix the mortar of fraternal time
with the dust of idols

Brussels, June 1939

SALES NÈGRES

Eh bien voilà :
nous autres
les nègres
les niggers
les sales nègres
nous n'acceptons plus
c'est simple
fini
d'etre en Afrique
en Amérique
vos nègres
vos niggers
vos sales nègres
nous n'acceptons plus
ça vous étonne
de dire : oui missié
en cirant vos bottes
oui mon pé
aux missionnaires blancs
ou maître
en récoltant pour vous
la canne à sucre
le café
le coton
l'arachide
en Afrique

FILTHY NEGROES

Well, it's like this:
we others
negroes
niggers
filthy negroes
we won't take anymore
that's right
we're through
being in Africa
in America
your negroes
your niggers
your filthy negroes
we won't take anymore
that surprises you
to say: *yessuh*
while polishing your boots
oui mon pé
to the white missionaries
or *master*
while harvesting your
sugar cane
coffee
cotton
peanuts
in Africa

en Amérique
en bons nègres
en pauvres nègres
en sales nègres
que nous étions
que nous ne serons plus
Fini vous verrez bien
nos yes Sir
oui blanc
sí Señor
        et
garde à vous, tirailleur
oui, mon Commandant,
quand on nous donnera l'ordre
de mitrailler nos frères Arabes
en Syrie
en Tunisie
au Maroc
et nos camarades blancs grévistes
crevant de faim
opprimés
spoliés
méprisés comme nous
les nègres
les niggers
les sales nègres

Surprise
quand l'orchestre dans vos boîtes

in America
like good negroes
poor negroes
filthy negroes
that we were
that we won't be anymore
We're finished you'll see
our *Yes Sir*
our *oui blanc*
our *sí Señor*
    and
attention, sharpshooter
oui, mon Commandant
when they order us
to machine gun our Arab brothers
in Syria
in Tunisia
in Morocco
and our white comrades on strike
starving to death
oppressed
plundered
despised like us
negroes
niggers
filthy negroes

Surprise
when the rhumba and blues bands

à rumbas et à blues
vous jouera tout autre chose
que n'attendait la putainerie blasée
de vos gigolos et salopes endiamantées
pour qui un nègre
n'est qu'un instrument
à chanter, n'est-ce pas,
à danser, of course
à forniquer naturlich
rien qu'une denrée
à acheter à vendre
sur le marché du plaisir
rien qu'un nègre
un nigger
un sale nègre

Surprise
jésusmariejoseph
surprise
quand nous attraperons
en riant effroyablement
le missionnaire par la barbe
pour lui apprendre à notre tour
à coups de pieds au cul
que
nos ancêtres
ne sont pas
des Gaulois
que nous nous foutons

in your clubs
start playing another rhythm
to accompany the blasé whoring
of your pimps and your diamond-studded sluts
for whom a negro
is but an instrument
for singing, n'est-ce pas,
for dancing, of course,
for fornicating, naturlich
no more than a commodity
to be bought and sold
on the pleasure market
no more than a negro
a nigger
a filthy negro

Surprise
jesusmary&joseph
surprise
when laughing frightfully
we will grab
the missionary by the beard
when it's our turn to teach him
with kicks in the ass
that
our ancestors
are not
Gauls
that we don't give a damn

d'un Dieu qui
s'il est le Père
eh bien alors c'est que nous autres
les nègres
les niggers
les sales négres
font croire que nous ne sommes que ses bâtards
et inutile de gueuler
jésusmariejoseph
comme une vieille outre de mensonges débondée
il faut bien
que nous t'apprenions
ce qu'il coûte en définitive
de nous prêcher à coups de chicote et de confiteors
l'humilité
la résignation
à notre sort maudit
de nègres
de niggers
de sales nègres

Les machines à écrire mâcheront les ordres de répression
en claquant des dents
fusillez
pendez
égorgez
ces nègres
ces niggers
ces sales nègres

about a God who
if he is our Father
well then it must be that we others
negroes
niggers
filthy negroes
make believe that we are only his bastards
and it's useless to shout
jesusmary&joseph
like an old goatskin canteen pouring out lies
it is necessary
we teach you
what it finally costs
to preach to us with horsewhips and cat-o-nine-tails
about humility
about submission
to our wretched lot
of negroes
niggers
filthy negroes

Clacking their teeth
typewriters will chew out orders of repression
shoot
hang
butcher
these negroes
these niggers
these filthy negroes

Englués comme des mouches à viande affolées
dans la toile d'araignée des graphiques de
cours de bourse effondrés
les gros actionnaires des compagnies minières et forestières
les propriétaires de rhumeries et de plantations
les propriétaires
de nègres
de niggers
de sales nègres
et la TSF délirera
au nom de la civilisation
au nom de la religion
au nom de la latinité
au nom de Dieu
au nom de la Trinité
au nom de Dieu nom de Dieu
des troupes
des avions
des tanks
des gaz
contre ces nègres
ces niggers
ces sales nègres

Trop tard
jusqu'au cœur des jungles infernales
retentira précipité le terrible bégaiement
télégraphique des tam-tams répétant infatigables
répétant

Caught like panic-stricken meat flies
in the spider web of graphs and charts
of collapsing market prices
fatcat stockholders of mining and lumber companies
owners of rum distilleries and plantations
owners
of negroes
niggers
filthy negroes
and the radio will rave on and on
in the name of civilization
in the name of religion
in the name of Latinity
in the name of God
in the name of the Holy Trinity
in the name of God in God's name
about the troops
planes
tanks
gas
launched against those negroes
those niggers
those filthy negroes

Too late
deep into the heart of infernal jungles
will throb the terrible telegraphic beating
of the tom-toms tirelessly beating beating
beating

que les nègres
n'acceptent plus
n'acceptent plus
d'être vos niggers
vos sales nègres
trop tard
car nous aurons surgi
des cavernes de voleurs des mines d'or du Congo
et du Sud-Afrique
trop tard il sera trop tard
pour empêcher dans les cotonneries de Louisiane
dans les Centrales sucrières des Antilles
la récolte de vengeance
des nègres
des niggers
des sales nègres
il sera trop tard je vous dis
car jusqu'aux tam-tams auront appris le langage
de l'Internationale
car nous aurons choisi notre jour
le jour des sales nègres
des sales indiens
des sales hindous
des sales indo-chinois
des sales arabes
des sales malais
des sales juifs
des sales prolétaires

that the negroes
won't take anymore
won't take anymore
being your niggers
your filthy negroes
too late
for we will have risen
from the thieves' dens from the gold mines in the Congo
and South Africa
too late it will be too late
on the cotton plantations of Louisiana
in the sugar cane fields of the Antilles
to halt the harvest of vengeance
of the negroes
the niggers
the filthy negroes
it will be too late I tell you
for even the tom-toms will have learned the language
of the *Internationale*
for we will have chosen our day
day of the filthy negroes
filthy Indians
filthy Hindus
filthy Indo-Chinese
filthy Arabs
filthy Malays
filthy Jews
filthy proletarians

Et nous voici debout
Tous les damnés de la terre
tous les justiciers
marchant à l'assaut de vos casernes
et de vos banques
comme une forêt de torches funèbres
pour en finir
une
    fois
        pour
            toutes
avec ce monde
de nègres
de niggers
de sales nègres

And here we are arisen
All the wretched of the earth
all the upholders of justice
marching to attack your barracks
your banks
like a forest of funeral torches
to be done
once
      and
          for
             all
with this world
of negroes
niggers
filthy negroes

NOUVEAU SERMON NÈGRE

À Tristan Rémy

Ils ont craché à Sa Face leur mépris glacé
Comme un drapeau noir flotte au vent battu par la neige
Pour faire de lui le pauvre nègre le dieu des puissants
De ses haillons des ornements d'autel
De son doux chant de misère
De sa plainte tremblante de banjo
Le tumulte orgueilleux de l'orgue
De ses bras qui halaient les lourds chalands
Sur le fleuve Jourdain
L'arme de ceux qui frappent par l'épée
De son corps épuisé comme le nôtre dans les plantations de coton
Tel un charbon ardent
Tel un charbon ardent dans un buisson de roses blanches
Le bouclier d'or de leur fortune
Ils ont blanchi Sa Face noire sous le crachat de leur
mépris glacé

Ils ont craché sur Ta Face noire
Seigneur, notre ami, notre camarade
Toi qui écartas du visage de la prostituée
Comme un rideau de roseaux ses longs cheveux
sur la source de ses larmes

NEW NEGRO SERMON

To Tristan Rémy

They spat their icy scorn in His Face
Like a black flag waving in the snow-battered wind
To make of Him the poor negro the god of the almighty
Of his rags altar vestments
Of his misery's sweet song
Of his banjo's quivering moan
The arrogant thunder of the organ
Of his arms that hauled heavy barges
On the River Jordan
The weapon of those who live by the sword
Of his body like ours beaten down on cotton plantations
Like a live coal
a live coal in a white rosebush
The gold shield of their fortune
They whitened His black Face with the spit of their
icy scorn

They spat in Your black Face
Lord, our friend, our comrade
You who pushed back from the whore's face
Her long hair like a curtain of reeds
covering the source of her tears

Ils ont fait
     les riches les pharisiens les propriétaires fonciers
                            les banquiers
Ils ont fait de l'Homme saignant le dieu sanglant
Oh Judas ricane
Oh Judas ricane :
Christ entre deux voleurs comme une flamme déchirée
au sommet du monde
Allumait la révolte des esclaves
Mais Christ aujourd'hui est dans la maison des voleurs
Et ses bras déploient dans les cathédrales l'ombre étendue
du vautour
Et dans les caves des monastères le prêtre compte les
intérêts des trente deniers
Et les clochers des églises crachent la mort sur les
multitudes affamées

Nous ne leur pardonnerons pas car ils savent ce
qu'ils font
Ils ont lynché John qui organisait le syndicat
Ils l'ont chassé comme un loup hagard avec des chiens
à travers bois
Ils l'ont pendu en riant au tronc du vieux sycomore
Non, frères, camarades
Nous ne prierons plus
Notre révolte s'élève comme le cri de l'oiseau de tempête
au-dessus du clapotement pourri des marécages
Nous ne chanterons plus les tristes spirituals désespérés
Un autre chant jaillit de nos gorges

They made
    the rich the pharisees the landowners
                the bankers
They made of bleeding Man the bloody god
Oh Judas snickers
Oh Judas snickers:
Christ between two thieves like a flame reviled
at the summit of the world
Ignited the revolt of the slaves
But Christ today is in the den of thieves
And his arms outstretched in cathedrals cast the vulture's
shadow
And in the catacombs the priest compounds the interest on
thirty pieces of silver
And the church belfries spit death on the starving
multitudes

We will not forgive them for they know what they do
They lynched John who organized the union
They chased him with dogs like a haggard wolf
through the woods
They laughed as they hung him from the trunk of the old sycamore
No, brothers, comrades
We will pray no more
Our revolution rises up like the cry of the stormbird
above the putrid lapping of swamps
No more will we sing sad despairing spirituals
Another song springs from our throats

Nous déployons nos rouges drapeaux
Tachés du sang de nos justes
Sous ce signe nous marcherons
Sous ce signe nous marchons
Debout les damnés de la terre
Debout les forçats de la faim

We go unfurling our red banners
Stained with the blood of our just
Under this sign we will march
Under this sign we are marching
Arise ye wretched of the earth
Arise ye prisoners of starvation

POETRY AS A WEAPON

An inquiry into the future of poetry is needed. Poetry is part of the ideological system whose multiple facets — psychology, art, ethics, philosophy, religion or spirituality — together reflect concrete historical reality.

Poetry is neither an idealist speculation nor a magical spell. Poetry is the reflection of what we commonly refer to as a historical era; that is, the dialectical complexity of social relations and contradictions within a given political-economic structure at a determined moment in history. Such a condition provides an element of analysis of this society.

An ambitious title for this essay might have been "From Mallarmé to Mayakovsky." The case of the great French poet seen alongside the revolutionary Russian poet illustrates clearly, in my view, what I am attempting to demonstrate.

Mallarmé appeared during a historical era when the political left's luck had already run out. Bourgeois society was in decline, adding to the destruction of the forces of production the wholesale rejection of cultural values.

If, from this death struggle, the writer gathers but a negative spirit and if, in the death of the crumbling social organism, the poet does not obtain an enduring social alternative of a higher order, then his fear and desperation are translated into an escape from reality capable of adopting the most varied forms.

I escape and seek my refuge at the crossroads
where one turns their back on life . . .

sings Mallarmé. And to facilitate his flight from reality is the solitary construction of a very strange poetics: an alchemical architecture of language and a kind of fanatic obsession with pure sound.

But this reinvention of language is not purely an aesthetic exercise: one can perceive in this a deliberate attempt to deny the commonplace by refusing to understand it.

Language is no stranger to the class struggle. For example, the development of social forces is easily traced from the 17th century to the French Revolution through the study of the poetics of stereotypical paraphrases designed to escape the everyday, the plebian, the popular, and through the exclusion or inclusion of certain words that clearly demonstrate the movements of the ruling class. Observed from this standpoint, Mallarmé's poetry is among the most reactionary known.

Paul Valéry exposes the attitude of the poet who isolates himself from the people:

"It does not displease the minority," he says, "to be the minority."

Happily, Valéry finds Mallarmé to be the least primitive of the poets who "give the impression — through an unusual and strangely sonorous coupling of drug-like words and through the musical splendor of verses and their singular plenitude — of that most powerful of elements in original poetry: the magic formula."

It is to acknowledge defeat if all the resources of our intelligence, the alliance of syntax with the most refined thought, and the desperate search for pure poetic expression lead us inevitably to the "synthesis of primitive magic."

Bourgeois society in decline must concoct this magical potion by mixing together concrete reality with intuitionism and a Bergsonian vital impulse. It is as if the exploration of the most elaborate forms of musical art has transported us backwards by means of a kind of paleontology from a Bach fugue to the archaic theme of the primitive drum.

There is, however, one fact that distinguishes Mallarmé from those poets and writers of today who are the architects of unreal thought: Mallarmé in his time was excluded and ridiculed by what we can term the well-bred literary society — the Academy, the bourgeois critics, the intellectual pillars of capitalism — while today those same denizens of the literary world greet with open arms the protagonists of the irrational and the dervishes of spiritualism.

What has happened is that, in the interim, the world has arrived at a crossroads where the forces of capitalism and socialism confront each other in a decisive struggle.

On the eve of this social transformation, the old collapsing society bows its head before metaphysical idols, retreats into the otherworldly forces of mysticism, and safeguards the counterrevolution's ideological weapons within idealist structures.

With an ethnologist's scientific scrutiny, we must examine those individuals who invent moral pretexts for entering by the kitchen door the camp of the people's enemies. When we do this, we discover the deplorable "petty bourgeois" insects, paralyzed by abject anguish, who take refuge in the chrysalis of pure poetry or in the liberation of the spirit, because history's unrelenting movement threatens the class interests of poetry's patrons who have commodified all mental production.

Above all, it is necessary to be done once and for all with the myth of the poet's freedom. Far from being a "very old man," as Valéry claimed, the poet is a contemporary being, the consciousness of his historical era. If his thought does not translate into action, the poet is not free. He is not free if he does not oblige himself to make imperative choices: to choose between García Lorca and General Franco, between Hitler and Thaelman, between peace and war, between socialist democracy and fascism. His alleged freedom ends in a kind of Pontius Pilot complex in which every artifice of the traitor's cowardice is at work. The poet is both witness and actor in the historical drama, and he is enlisted into this drama with full responsibility. And particularly in our time, his art must be a frontline weapon in the service of the people.

I realize that many people will become indignant that such a mission be assigned to the poet. For them, the poet's place is among the transcendent spheres of the spirit: while the destiny of man is played out amidst tremendous social and historical upheaval, he is able to withdraw into the private property of spiritual solitude and continue to write comic songs balanced between the traditional poles of the erotic and the dream.

The moral law of the spirit is human necessity. One of the most admirable things I find in Lenin's work is that the author of dialectical materialism, of empirical criticism, this encyclopediac spirit, this giant of poetry, wrote a pamphlet demanding that the workers in Schulusselburg's textile mills be given boiled water to make tea. And Mayakovsky answered to the poet's true revolutionary call when he put his art at the service of the anti-typhus struggle.

Today, the poet's art must be a weapon taking the form of a leaflet, a pamphlet or a poster. If, in poetry, we can unite beauty, form and class consciousness, if we can deep down learn the lessons of Mayakovsky, we will be able to create a great revolutionary poetry in defense of the human spirit.

— *Cahiers d'Haiti 1944*